Private Eye

Private Eye

poems by Wendy Morton

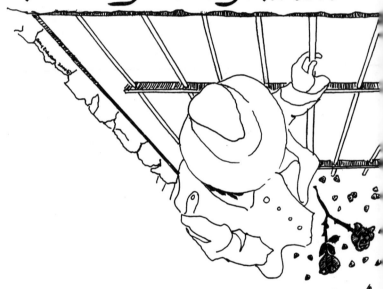

Private Eye

Wendy Morton

*To Anita & Sean,
with love and
delight
from Wendy*

Ekstasis Editions

National Library of Canada Cataloguing in Publication Data

Morton, Wendy, 1940-
  Private eye

Poems.
ISBN 1-896860-91-5

I. Title.
PS8576.O778P74 2001   C811'.6   C2001-910160-0
PR9199.3.M657P74 2001

© Wendy Morton, 2001.
Cover Photos: Karen Connelly
Frontispiece drawing: Amy Zidulka

Acknowledgements:
Some of the poems in this book have appeared in the following magazines: *The Antigonish Review, CVII, Other Voices, Zygote* and *grain.* Other poems have appeared in three chapbooks published by *Outlaw Editions: Community of Monsters, Blindfolds,* and *Other Abductions.*

  Steven Heighton's wonderful poem, "Psalm: Hands of the Beautiful Swimmers" inspired my poem, "Beautiful Hands". James Bertolino's "Toast", which opens this book, acts as a benediction.

  These poems owe much to the encouragement and love of my companion, Rod Punnett, and to the inspiration of Patrick Lane, who has taught me to listen to the wind inside my mind. I'd like to thank the audiences at Mocambopo, who listened to these poems on Friday nights and let me know when they liked them. To name the poets whose words have moved and delighted me, I would have to make a list that would stretch across the outline of blue hills.

Published in 2001 by:
Ekstasis Editions Canada Ltd.
Box 8474, Main Postal Outlet
Victoria, B.C. V8W 3S1

Ekstasis Editions
Box 571
Banff, Alberta T0L 0C0

THE CANADA COUNCIL | LE CONSEIL DES ARTS
FOR THE ARTS | DU CANADA
SINCE 1957 | DEPUIS 1957

BRITISH
COLUMBIA
ARTS COUNCIL
Supported by the Province of British Columbia

Private Eye has been published with the assistance of a grant from the Canada Council for the Arts and the Cultural Services Branch of British Columbia.

Dedication

This book is dedicated to my companion, Rod Punnett and to Wallace Francis Xavier McPhee, my oldest friend on the earth. And to the lovely ghosts whose spirits are honoured in these poems.

The Toast

May you always have art to charm
your days, a sensible hearth
and friends as dependable as gravity.
May the wind and creatures be as music
to your evenings alone, and may your dreams
leave you renewed. May you have an appaloosa
to ride the outline of blue hills, and nothing
that sickens, and no black sticks.

James Bertolino © 1983

CONTENTS

STREAMING FLAMINGOS

Poems are everywhere;
starry, ephemeral, delicious,
for the eating.
Take for instance,
the cyclist
with a pink flamingo aloft,
streaming with iridescent ribbons,
a sunlit metaphor.
Or the skateboard guy
with a suit and flowering tie
all grace and light,
simply on his way to work.
Or the gift of a recipe for pumpkin soup:
take a pumpkin,
fill it with broth,
potatoes, carrots, thyme.
Bake it.
Eat this poem.

PATISSERIE DANIEL

We are appropriate matrons,
waiting patiently in line at Daniel's
as if we were waiting for our lovers.

Still and perfumed,
imaginations alive,
we wait for:
sweet potato gorgonzola pie,
hazelnut, roasted onion and pear rolls,
French goat cheese with pistachios,
olive, onion, tomato brioche
double chocolate bread,
blackberry and Frangipan delight.

This is better than love,
as succulent and sticky,
and even two for one.

FLYING WITH FRANK

You can't fly, you can't fly,
my mother used to say.
I only heard her last word.
I wanted to be airborne, winged.
I nearly flew at any chance,
on roller skates, on new ice.
I even tried glissandos on the beach.

But Frank Walters really flew.
In 1982 he bought
an orange Sears and Roebuck lawn chair,
42 weather balloons,
55 cylinders of helium,
a package of beef jerky,
a road map of California,
and 2 litres of Coca-Cola.
He wanted to see the Mojave desert, flying.

One blue day he floated high,
over 259 shopping malls,
5,373 swimming pools and
92 used car lots.
He reached 16,500 feet;
his toes froze,
his heart opened,
he saw the desert glow.

He was spotted by the pilot of TWA flight 231:
"We have a man in a chair,
attached to balloons."
He was fined by the FAA
for dreaming,
for flying unauthorized
into his dream.

My mother was wrong.
I've flown with Frank,
felt the ice wind high above the desert;
have flown unauthorized
into my dreams.

WINGS
for Bill Lishman

Wild Bill could lasso his dreams;
bring them to ground
like a cowboy roping a calf.

He wanted to build Stonehenge
in ice and rusted car parts;
build a space capsule,
a cement house
like an underground ship.
The dreamer sailed into his dreams.

But the best of all
were the geese
who imprinted on him
and his goose-shaped ultralight.

When they flew with him
he said he had no more dreams,
that was it;
his turning into something
he could only imagine.

He became mother goose,
father goose,
and dreamed,
when the geese flew beside him,
that he had grown wings.

DAY FOR NIGHT

The checkout girl at the Superstore
says, "have a good night".
I check my watch.
It's 10 a.m.
I wonder if she's being existential?
Maybe she's seen Truffaut's *Day for Night*
and is making a statement about shifting
        reality planes.

I've just bought bananas for 29 cents a pound
and am filled with guilt, thinking of
the Equadorian peasants who pick them;
I am worried about the ash
in the cheap cat food I buy.
I am undone by the thought
of irradiation;
genetic engineering.
Maybe I should write a letter.

I want life to be simpler.
I want this checkout angel
to spread her tattooed wings
and tell me to have a good day
and watch the light shine from her
day or night.

At the Bank

The woman in front of me in line
pulled out a wad of
hundred dollar bills
that would, as my mother
used to say,
choke a horse.
She counted each bill out
in slow delight. Smiled.

She was nearly beautiful:
honey skinned,
honey blond,
wearing a white dress,
spaghetti strapped,
that ended thigh top,
shiny black patent leather
high heels,
vermilion nails.

The old fellow behind me,
wearing his British wool,
dropped his cane,
exclaimed, "it must be summer."

I watched her leave;
her summer body cut the air
like a cool knife.

I was wearing
my Coldwater Creek shirtdress,
my practical Israeli sandals,
my amazed and starry middle age.

I would not trade
her insistent, golden beauty,
or her hundred dollar bills,
for my familiar, vermilion scars.

Bernie's Wake

The News

He heard the doctor say Canfor, Cologne. Thought:
German logging.
Then he got it.
The black wave hit him head on.
Knocked his mind blank.

Cancer.

He went home, told the dog,
the cat, the passing moon, the ravens.
His wife already knew.

Then he called up his friends,
invited them to Buffy's Pub
for a practice wake;
just in case the real thing was close at hand.

The Wake

Bernie arrived at Buffy's Pub
wearing his opera cape lined in scarlet,
a silk cravat, his best blue blazer, a top hat.
He laid himself out on a table
and crossed his hands over his chest.

He asked his friends to be eloquent on his behalf;
suggested they mention:
his reticence and courage, his love of Mozart,
his abundant gardens, his house on the Point.
All that he loved:
his wife, his children, his friends, his dog, his cats,
the koi in the pond,
the seasons of his dreams.

Be specific he said,
give death something delicious to eat.

Post Op

Bernie stood in the supermarket,
holding a can of Campbell's Tomato Soup.
Then he showed me
where they'd take the nodes from his lungs
in a month.

He reached for the organic macaroni,
said he was on soft foods until
his colon healed.

He said, "I sleep alot,
have raging dreams,
hear Mozart in my head.
I wake up and think I'm singing."

I said, "It's life's Sirens' singing.
Listen, listen

Listen.

FRED, I NEED YOU
for Ward Kruse

This was supposed to be a poem about Fred,
who asks the strippers he meets in bars
to sign his best red overalls.
He carries their pictures
clipped to his waist,
where they wait, like small poems:
Ginger Sincere,
Coco Rico,
Millenia,
Wild Orchid.
"Fred," they write,
"I need you."

Then a friend's letter arrived
with these red words:
"Diagnosed,
lymph nodes,
radiation."

Fred, I need you,
to raise your glass
of black heart oatmeal stout
and give a toast
to life's red surprises,
to cancer's wild orchids,
to my friend
and his brave, stout, hopeful heart.

MY FRIENDS DIE
for Shirley Atkinson

My friends die.
I see them in the thin blue light
of hospital rooms,
where they lie,
newly scarred,
their lambent dreams,
beyond reach.

Entubed,
fluids move
through them,
from them.
Later, they become
brave, hairless,
radiant.

I discover their photographs
in drawers,
smiling, distracted by life,
or caught in conversation,
in blurry pixilation
as they move
toward the last blue light.

KATHLEEN'S HAT
for Kathleen Ryan

Kathleen died at Equinox,
after the bright summer
she learned how to die.

She sat, facing the Strait,
the smell of seaweed and roses
on the wind.
Her face, a pale rose,
turned to the sun.
She watched the gulls
circle and glide.

"This is it, honey, the real thing,"
she said.

She leaned into me,
for heat, for life.
I held her hand,
read old poems,
told jokes, juggled words,
while the roses of cancer
bloomed in her.

I still want to call her up,
tell her secrets,
bring her Stargazer lilies
and Gravenstein apples.

I wear Kathleen's sensible straw hat
and think of her,
think of her
blooming
at Equinox.

CIRCUS, BURNING
for Rick, flying
for Chris, dreaming

You dream you are in the big tent,
clowns tumble,
juggle knives.
You watch the man
on the flying trapeze
and you catch your breath,
catching him in flight
and flying,
you watch the tent
burst into beautiful flames
while the orchestra plays.
Death, wearing a clown's mask,
smiles.

Between dreams
you watched his mind die fast,
burning.
And some nights
you sat by him in the quiet room
and told him you'd miss him,
miss everything.

The night you dreamt
of burning tents
you woke knowing
that when his breathing stopped,
death, that heartbreak clown,
would start juggling.

DEATH'S NECKLACE
for Rooth Cross

My friend wears death's necklace,
she says she thinks of white butterflies
flying in her blood.
She is hopeful:
she will plant a garden,
plan a picnic,
dance.
One breast is gone,
now half a colon,
the lymph nodes next.

There should be ceremonies
for her parts:
ritual burials;
celebrations with
incantations and incense.
Instead,
there are the blurred words
of oncologists,
the lies of friends,
death's transparent, burning wings.

Dear Sylvia

"Dying is an art
like everything else,
I do it exceptionally well"
                    — Sylvia Plath

The sheets on your bed
had hospital corners.
In your kitchen
the jars labelled
sugar, flour, coffee, tea
were always full.
No one found dust
under tables, chairs.
Instead they found you
cornered by your jars
and dustless rooms.
You had often dreamed of death;
mapped it out,
asked oblique questions
of mechanics, pharmacists,
hid your pills in the back corner
of a drawer, inside a velvet bag.
Your arranged precise backups:
a flexible metal hose
rolled up in the garage,
razor blades
in the blue teapot.
Was anything enough?

What is enough for us, poets
who write poems on our hands?
We want magic,
poems that burn.

Sylvia.

One day you forgot
the names on the labels of the jars
forgot your last poem
reached for the velvet bag
at the back of the drawer
at the back of the drawer
and died well
with exceptions.

STARLINGS

The starlings that live between
the Sussex building and the CIBC
take up the sky with wings and cries.

They stir the day:
mix it up with insistence;
black against the light.

I think of the man who
complained of flights of the mind
and walked one day
into the Strait and drowned.

His mind, I imagine,
moved like the starlings
like breathing
like stars;
more movement
than he could hold
when he walked into the cold
indifferent dark.

91 Degrees

In Palm Springs it is 91 degrees.
There is drought forecast,
fires in the desert.
In the Santa Rosa Mountains,
in the palm canyons of Agua Caliente,
the heat swells the day.

You call to tell me you're bleeding in Palm Springs;
that you're a roadmap of tubes and fear:
your voice sings on the far edge of death.

I want to call Chihuly up,
the man who built an ice wall in Jerusalem.
Bring him blocks of ice, I'd tell Chihuly,
build an ice wall outside his hospital room.
Block on block,
build a wall
of clear ice dreams
so he could watch it melt
into his heart's cartography:
into its crossroads of joy,
into its roadways of light,
into the burning canyons of his life.

Ice Child

In the high Andes,
in the Inca ruins,
a child was buried.
She wore a woven shawl, a silver pin,
a necklace of ruby shells.
In her frozen hands
she held a golden doll.
She was eight years old.
Five hundred years later,
lightning found her,
moved deep into the earth,
burned her.

And I think of how she died,
a sacrificed child,
how the priests gave her *chicha*,
made her drunk,
then lay her in the wind to die.
Singing, they buried her
with a silver llama
and a coca bag of orange feathers.

Later, scientists
wearing latex gloves
would test her DNA,
do needle biopsies,
search for antibodies,
keep her perfect organs frozen.

They would miss
her perfect hands,
the poetry of her,
the songs she never sang,
this child,
this child of ice and lightning.

S-21

The S-21 pictures, taken by Khmer Rouge soldiers and preserved along with written confessions as an official record of execution, comprise one of the most powerful and heart-rending photographic documents of genocide in the twentieth century.

Kyo Maclear,

Saturday Night

I want to turn my eyes away,
find instead a blown crimson rose or
a blue bowl of oranges in sunlight.
But my mind has fixed
the image of this Cambodian child;
tagged with the number one,
an iron chain around his neck.

Was he chained first,
this boy,
death already in his eyes?

Who took this picture,
wrote this child's name,
gave him a rusted shovel,
shot him,
burst his crimson heart?

What words are there
for this chained child,
what words?

THE SANDWOMEN

One must have a mind of winter
To regard the frost and the boughs
Of the pinetrees crusted with snow;
And have been cold a long time.
        Wallace Stevens, "The Snow Man"

The women of Mali come out of the darkness
bearing bowls of sand;
they clear the courtyards
until the wind blows off the Sahara
from the eastern dunes;
then they stop in the sand's glitter,
still as shadows, wrapped in black.
One must have a mind of winter

to stay. The sandwomen dream
on the mind's horizon,
with the immutable grace of gazelles;
they dream of high meadows,
cold bright oceans, foam's lace,
rain   rain.
They wait
to regard the frost and the boughs

of their winter dreams.
Sand sweeps in again.
They pick up their bowls,
move into the courtyards,
move off a distance and return
to begin, begin, begin
until the dreams begin
of pinetrees crusted with snow.

Caravans move
through the village, carrying salt.
The women stop, lean from the doorways,
watch the traders' eyes on them.
If the wind is still they can smell the salt
from the inland sea.
They know these winter dreams
and have been cold a long time.

BRIDES, DIVING

In the Santa Rosa sunlight,
the bride dives,
her veil trailing.
The second before she hits the water
she knows
that she will ruin everything;
that love will leave her
and find her again because
she is someone's wife
wearing a white dress and diamonds.
She will swim under water,
a white mermaid,
the wife of someone,
diving.

* * * *

In Jalalabad,
40 miles west of the Kyber Pass,
the woman, wearing a green burka,
shows her broken hands.
The Taliban, she says,
saw her painted nails
and beat her,
beat her.

No one can see her,
but she sees the world
in squares of brilliant light.
In her mind
she dives into blue water,
wearing a white dress and ruined hands,
knowing she is the wife of someone,
dying.

The Bones of Tusla

Under the solstice moon
I imagined heartbreak or magic.
My mind turned glowing
to the tunnels of Tusla,
where 2000 bodies,
all rags and bones,
wait in the dark to be found.

Sophia Ivankovic
waits outside the tunnels of Tusla,
under this solstice moon.
She knows her husband's bones are there;
she imagines she hears his heart beat.

She has answered the questions
on duplicate forms:
what colour was his shirt: silver
was it torn: yes
were there any broken bones:
his wrist, broken as a child.

Sophia stands under the moon,
silver, torn, broken
as a child,
listening, listening,
to the solstice bones.

Kosovo

In my dream
they arrive at my door;
their broken hearts in their eyes,
the shards of their lives
wrapped in old coats.

They do not speak.
The men weep,
the children are voiceless.

It is the wrong season.

I run to the garden,
find leeks, potatoes, kale.
Make a soup.

I give them warm scarves.
They show me old photographs,
new scars.

I wake
as they arrive at my door.

The Wells

In the wells of Kosovo
are the bodies of women
layered like grotesque parfaits.

I want them to have died first
and quickly.
My mind turns away from them,
these bodies,
layered with grey blankets.

The shape of hips
arms
breasts
in the red water,
under the blankets of grief
in the poisoned wells,
in the ruined villages.
In Kosovo,
drowning.

KITKATLA

Maria calls me friend,
she does not know my name.

"Friend," she says, "we were people of the salt.
There were totems, gone, now, gone
all burned.
And the booze is bad,
it took my sons,
took my husband,
he was the keeper of the songs,
my daughter too, Raven, drowned,
drowned.
I raise her son,
now he's found the booze,
him too, I think,
what can I do?
I hold him every day,
call him Raven son.
He calls me mom."

I hear Maria.
Hear the cold salt rain in her words
that hangs in the grey curtain of clouds
over Kitkatla.

"Friend," I say,
"friend."

CONVERSATION AT THE SUPERSTORE

I see that the picture of the woman with 3 hearts on the
cover of the National Enquirer is a triple exposure.
                              — Woman in line

She tells me that she is leaving for Scotland,
for an equestrian tour of the Highlands;
a long dream.

"I want to ride over the moors," she says,
"see castles in the mist."

She imagines Heathcliff,
in triple exposure, calling her from the moor,
watching her ride,
dream over dream.

And I think of Heathcliff,
how he gathered heather in his arms,
all love and madness.
How he sang into the mist
with heartbreak and sorrow;
over and over and over
for any rider to hear.

MAGIC

Isn't
the circus poster woman who defies time
as she ages to a skeleton
and turns into an enormous snake.

Is
the hard seed
that springs like a dancer
toward life,
flings its leaves,
sings into sunlight,
blooms.
Like love,
that spins around corners,
catches the heart off guard.

Magic is
agate, jasper,
obsidian, phosphoria,
columbine, lobelia,
aubretia.
Stone. Flowers of the heart.

BEAUTIFUL HANDS

The man on the train has beautiful hands
He tells me he knows magic,
juggling, classical equitation.

He shows me an iridescent glass heart.
Tells me to hold it to the light
to see my bones:
lunate, hamate, metacarpal, phalange.

I lay the heart in my open palm
watch my bones glow,
my hand burn.

Magic, he says,
magic.

The man on the train has beautiful hands.
He tells me how he charts the stars,
knows the phases of the moon,
plants gardens
of basil, shallot, sage and chard.

He is guarded, elliptical,
safe as summer.

He already knows I have a glass heart,
beautiful scars,
magic.

YOUR MOTHER'S HANDS

You have your mother's hands.
Like raven's wings, they shape the air,
are lovely in flight.

Your mother's hands
smell of oranges and clay;
she can catch the wind
in her singing mind.

She knows that
1000 clematis grew
outside her door last summer.

She can draw horses.
She has secrets.
From her you learned
to climb the wind,
risk foolishness,
imagine circuits, systems,
fix everything.
Fly with raven's wings.

PLUM TREES

The plum trees are in bloom
in opulent cascade
this first spring day
I miss you,
miss
the blooming trees
our opulent
silent
bloom

WHISTLING

In the high Arctic,
if you whistle,
the Northern Lights
fall into your hands
like the music of an
Appalachian dulcimer.

This is how I imagine love must be:
this familiar shimmer and flash.
But in the night sky
the light falls into your hands;
you can play it like love,
nearly touch it
as it falls,
as you fall
whistling
into the light.

PAS DE DEUX

for Tanya Kern

You dance a *pas de deux*
wearing your best sadness
and a blue dress.
Your ghost lover
tries to catch
the pieces of your singing heart
that rush into the air;
small vermillion birds.
They land in formal gardens,
on rusted swings,
onto the wings of a varied thrush
and into the hands of someone who has not read your poems.

He takes it as a sign.
He does not know whose blood has touched him:
imagines a poet,
a ghost,
a lover,
dancing in blue.

New Orleans

I want to tell you
how random life is.

Take, for instance,
the blond who sat in the New Orleans bar
in only her mink coat
and how you got drunk,
got drunk on her soft words,
her honeyed skin.

Then your wife arrived,
taking for truth
what was true.
On the way home she wept,
broken.

Later, when a tree fell on you
you said the pain was easier to bear
than the long ride home,
years ago.

Sometimes,
on drunken summer nights,
when the air feels like mink
and your mind cracks,
your heart breaks,
your hands remember
New Orleans.

SHELLS

On Ko Sumet,
garlands of shells
hang from abandoned cabins;
the shells are twisted,
broken by the sea:
the various shapes of sorrow.

I cut one garland down
to remember the island,
the warm sea,
your insistent absence.
I held one smooth shell
against my wrist,
imagined I could draw blood,
write you one last poem
that you could understand.

No.

This is the last poem,
whose sorrow you will miss,
as you missed Ko Sumet,
the twisted shells, the golden sea.

MOTORCYCLE WIND

Motorcycle wind, sweet woodruff,
salt marsh,
columbine
    pine
resin: that summer I was fifteen
when I lay in the height mountain air
barely breathing.

There was so much love
I pressed my legs against you for words.

You took my picture,
lost it, lost words, lost

I handed out stars, supplications,
blue stones.

Rainbow Girls

The rainbow girls sit in the inner harbour
tattooed, iridescent,
with prismed mermaid's tails,
scallop shells for breasts.
They glisten, are resplendent.
They toss seaweed from their hair
as if they had arrived
unbidden from the sea
to dance with someone
who would make their hearts bloom
like a thousand roses
until the sea catches them
and they drown.

TO HEAL A BROKEN HEART

for Karen Connelly

Sing.
Sing a poem
while your heart
flies from your throat
like a silver bird.
Catch it.
Wrap it in old silk.

Find a Greek island,
a cabin in a field of lavender and sorrow.
Wait there   wait
for the jasmine wind
for the retsina wind.

When you hear the hooves
of a golden horse
hold your shining heart
in the broken light
and sing,
sing a poem.

CIRCLES

In the driveway, twelve winter wrens
foraged for fall seeds,
and suddenly rose,
circling on the wind
like a single breath.

Later, the alder leaves circled
like the winter birds.

And so I circle you
as you have circled me;
riding the wind
like a single breath.

SPRING CLEANING

Once, in early summer,
Mother, wearing burgundy lace,
danced with a stranger;
dancing and dancing into the starry night.
She was younger then
and not so much alone.

Years ago, she forgot his face,
the June starlight,
the moon's weight,
the air thick with rose.

Today, she cleans her closet,
packs her clothes in paper bags;
touches the leafy silk,
the shawls from Spain,
the long grey gown
with raglan sleeves
she never wore.

The hangers rattle.
She likes the sound,
the empty space,
the sense of having done the thing.

When the phone rings,
she folds her dreams in paper bags
and dancing, dancing,
moves into the light.

WEDDING PICTURE

My mother wears my dreaming face,
two orchids, a hat and veil,
sensible shoes.

She is a sensible bride,
an orchid bride, blooming
in a small room.

Twenty relatives
arranged in layers behind her
bless this day
with their bright, hard names:
Feingold,
Opperman,
Glicksman,
Freeman,
Fischgrund.

I want to reach into the picture,
take her hand,
tell her life will never be
so perfectly arranged again.

Death will leave her sitting
alone in this small room
and the smiling ghosts will bless her,
will bless her.

GRANDMA, DANCING

When Grandma was sixty-five
she could touch her toes,
bending from the waist.
And dance, hairpins flying;
a gypsy under the burning moon.

Then she'd pour herself a sherry,
put her apron on,
and make a steaming dish of chicken paprikash.

Grandma, I carry you in my apron pocket.
I make your lentil soup:
eggplant, apricots,
a little cinnamon to taste.

Grandma, I know your
steaming Hungarian ghost burns in me:
the cook,
the dancer, dancing,
bending from the waist.

POET, LEAVING
for Patrick Lane

You call to tell me that you're leaving town.
You're not a man who likes to leave,
you like things as they are:
the imperfect arrangement of books on shelves,
the predictable shadows of plum trees.
You are leaving
this hesitant fall,
as the leaves hang gilded, still.
You are leaving,
there is no time for celebration.

If you would stay awhile,
I would make fusilli,
with eggplant and golden peppers,
and red bell peppers,
sweet onions, shining and peeled,
garlic, smelling of earth,
portabellos roasted in oil.

And you would remember
the smell of it
filling the kitchen
and you would leave,
hesitant, the smell of it
filling your poems.

FALLING BOUNDARY

I know this forest:
the nurse logs,
the windfalls, their beautiful moss,
the winter streams,
the winter pond,
the winter wrens.

I know the raven with tattered wings
who cries to the silent deer,
to the black bear I've never seen.

Blackberry forest,
salmonberry forest.
Maple, hemlock, balsam, fir.
I know this forest,
breathe it,
breathe it.

I know the machines with terrible names
that wait at the boundary:
grapple skidder,
crawler dozer,
feller buncher.

I know the wasteland they will leave:
the ruined steams,
the silted pond,
and the raven
    who cries.

FALLING WATER BIRDS

The red winged blackbirds
arrive each year
in the trees behind the house.
I call them
the falling water birds.
There is a stillness my mind remembers.
Not the sound of birds.
Waterfalls. Cascades of light.

What are the sounds
the mind makes? Falling water. Blackbirds.

MARGERY, COUNTING

Margery counted the morning glories
that bloomed outside her door.
She told us each one lasted only one short day.
Sixty times she watched them open,
opulent and blue,
then die.

She marked their shining life
in a book she keeps;
clematis, calendula,
wisteria, rue,
all entered;
each bloom pressed
to remember.

In our house she dusts, rearranges,
resurrects a whale bone,
a bird skull, a bleached shell
for us to see or see again.

Here she counts the windfall apples,
the boats on the Strait,
the winter wrens.

Margery watches,
counts everything,
to remember
all that is opulent, blue.

She Could Swim Like Esther Williams

In her good old days,
she could leap three feet in the air
to catch a stick,
her tail twirling
like a helicopter blade.
And she could swim
like Esther Williams.

I brought her home from the pound
in a shopping bag,
thought she's grow into a lab.
She stayed small, smart, persistent.
She cleaned the dirty pans,
learned to dance,
sat on my lap by the fire.

Then her eyes clouded,
her hearing went,
her legs gave out.
One day she couldn't make it
up the stairs.
She spent the night
under the blue wheelbarrow
waiting to be found.

We carried her inside,
put a hot water bottle by her,
fed her cookies and milk,
hovered.
In human years she was 110.

I called the vet.
When he saw her,
he said, "ah, she's so bright"
and kissed her on the lips.

I laid my hand on her head,
to catch her soul.
It took ten seconds for her to die.
When we buried her,
we threw in rosepetals,
her favorite stick,
pieces of our hearts.

TATTOOS

When Chelsea's grandpa died,
she had his name tattooed on her leg
to honour him, and for good measure
added her grandma's name,
her mom and dad's,
her own, her cat's.

So the list read:
Bernie
Fran
Carol
Roy
Chelsea
Tiger
and ended with a heart.

My own tattoos would take
a whole leg for the dead I've loved;
and for the living,
the rest of my limbs.

I'd have a heart tattooed
over my own heart
to cover the jagged edges that death leaves,
that life leaves
tattooed.

SLEEPING WITH THE SWANS

1.

Between poems,
I walk to the beach
to join the sleeping swans.
They are white and gilded.
I lay near them,
on the sharp stones,
so close that I can hear them sleep.
They make small singing sounds like cats dreaming.
Suddenly, they wake,
stretch in unison and preen;
winged dancers.

I close my eyes
and imagine this poem, sleeping,
between poems, as the swans sleep.

2.

I have written this poem
on the back of a grocery list.
When I hold the paper to the light
another poem shines through:

Penne, feta, artichokes,
garlic, salsa, beans,
sourdough bread.

It has nothing to do with sleep or swans,
because the swans arrived
between the poems,
between the words,
between the meals the list became.

Between East Pine & Arras

This is the dead land
between seasons,
between pulp mills
between Dawson Creek & Chetwyn.
The names on the highway signs
have hope, poetry:
East Pine,
Ground Birch,
Willow Valley,
Progress,
Sunset Prairie,
Arras.

I drive past gray farms,
black trees,
old snow.

Will this place bloom
with balsam,
black sage,
wild stock,
larkspur?

Between East Pine and Arras,
Progress, Sunset Prairie,
spring?

CALVES DANCING

On the road to McCleese Lake,
there are cows and calves
wandering the road.
Piebald, white faced,
mottled; peace washes
over them.

I stop, watch them move
through the grass;
steaming in dreamtime.

Frank Sinatra sings
on the radio:
"New York, New York",
I roll the window down,
turn the volume up.
The calves hear it
and leap.

I want to imagine
that life is always like this:
slow, ruminant,
random.
Calves dancing.

WAXWING MAGIC

Not just the wooden boats,
or the ancient gaff-rigged sails
moving into the Strait,
or the smell of a hundred coats
of marine enamel:
teal blue,
blue sea,
sea grey.

The captains, with skin like spar varnish,
these poet captains,
sail their wooden boats:
Summer wind,
Carina,
Deep leap
Dulcimer,
Waxwing,
Magic,

Rejoice.